Ladybird

A note for parents and teachers

Time, Seasons and Weather introduces young people
learning English to the important concepts of telling the
time, the days of the week, the months of the year,
the seasons and the many kinds of weather experienced
in different parts of the world.

A small cast of professional working characters
demonstrate the details of one twenty-four
hour day during a seven-day week, and then take us
through the months of the year, celebrating each in turn.
The seasons and weathers of the world
are then accurately described and colourfully illustrated.

The concepts are also listed at the end of the book
for ease of reference.

The *Time, Seasons and Weather Workbook* in this new
Ladybird series provides further practice in the
use of the concepts which have been learned in this
book, placing them in lively, stimulating activities,
puzzles and crosswords.

Further information on local Ladybird stockists
may be obtained from the International Sales Department
Ladybird Books Ltd Beeches Road Loughborough
Leicestershire LE11 2NQ UK
Telephone: + 44 509 268021   Fax: + 44 509 219158

A catalogue record for this book is available
from the British Library

Published by Ladybird Books Ltd Loughborough Leicestershire UK
Ladybird Books Inc Auburn Maine 04210 USA

Printed in the United Kingdom by Ladybird Books Ltd - Loughborough

Time
Seasons and
Weather

words by Valerie Mendes
pictures by John Lobban

Times of the day: Morning

At **seven o'clock** Liz gets ready for work.

At **five past eight** Harry arrives at school.

At **ten past nine** Tim stops the traffic.

At **quarter past eleven** Julie starts to cook.

Times of the day: Afternoon

At **twenty past twelve** Maggie practises her singing at the piano.

At **twenty-five past two** Chuck makes his exciting new movie.

At **half past three** Sheila paints a picture.

At **quarter to five** Alan arrives at the airport.

Times of the day: Evening

At **twenty to six** Liz finishes work at the hospital.

At **quarter to seven** Maggie practises with the band.

At **ten to eight** Tim watches television.

At **five to nine** Julie cleans her kitchen.

Times of the day: Night

At **midnight** Harry finishes marking papers.

At **twenty past one** Chuck goes to bed.

At **quarter past four** Sheila wakes up.

At **half past five** Alan flies his plane.

Days of the week

On **Monday** at twenty past one Julie serves lunch. She likes cooking for lots of people.

On **Tuesday** at ten past six Harry reads a book. Tomorrow he will read it to his class at school.

Days of the week

On **Wednesday** at quarter past ten Chuck
watches his movie in his small cinema.

On **Thursday** at three o'clock Sheila goes to an
art gallery to look at some paintings.

9

Days of the week

On **Friday** at half past seven Maggie sings in her concert. The audience clap and cheer.

On **Saturday** morning at eight o'clock Alan lands his plane. He is pleased to be home again.

Days of the week

On **Sunday** at one o'clock they all eat lunch together. Can you name each of them?

A Rhyme to Remember

A leap year has 366 days and happens once every four years.

Thirty days have September
April, June and November
All the rest have thirty-one
Except for February alone
Which has twenty-eight days clear
And twenty-nine in each leap year.

Months of the year

Maggie's birthday is in **January**.
When is your birthday?

In **February** Julie makes a birthday cake.
Do you like cake?

Alan puts lights on his trees in **March**.
What colours are they?

In **April** everyone sings "Happy Birthday!"
What do you sing?

13

Months of the year

Sheila receives lots of cards in **May**. Do you get birthday cards?

Liz ties some balloons to her door in **June**. How many are there?

Chuck has a big party in **July** for his friends. Do you like parties?

In **August** Tim puts three candles on a cake. How old is his daughter?

Months of the year

In **September** Julie has a barbecue. Do you like eating outdoors?

In **October** Harry takes the school photograph. Do you have one?

In **November** everyone wears party hats. Do you like hats?

Then in **December** Liz gives Alan a present. What do you think it is?

Seasons: Spring

In **spring** the snow melts. The days grow longer and warmer. Flowers bloom and fruit trees blossom. Birds sing and build nests for their young.

Seasons: Summer

In **summer** fruits ripen and the trees are green. The sun shines in a clear blue sky. The days are hot. At night you can see the moon and stars.

Seasons: Autumn

In **autumn** the leaves turn red and yellow and orange. They fall from the trees. The days get shorter and colder. The nights are damp and cool.

Seasons: Winter

In **winter** it is often very cold. Sometimes snow falls. There is frost on the windows. Water turns to ice. We wear woollen hats to keep warm.

Seasons: The dry season

In **the dry season** there is no rain for many weeks and months. The weather is hot and dry. There are few clouds in the sky. The grass is brown.

Seasons: The wet season

In **the wet season** rain falls every day. There are big clouds in the sky. There are puddles and mud on the ground. Plants grow big and green.

Weather: Sun

The **sun** keeps us warm. Too much sun makes us hot and we look for shade and wear cool clothes. When it is hot it is nice to go swimming.

Weather: Rain

We get wet when it rains. We use umbrellas to keep dry. Children like to play in **rain** puddles. Sometimes after rain we can see a rainbow.

Weather: Wind

When the **wind** blows, trees bend and the clouds race across the sky. Very strong winds are called gales, typhoons or hurricanes. They can even blow roofs off houses. A gentle wind is called a breeze.

24

Weather: Fog

When there is **fog** it is difficult to see. It is like being in the middle of a cloud. When it is foggy, cars use fog lights and ships use fog horns to find their way. Fog can be very dangerous.

Weather: Snow

When it is very cold in some countries, **snow** falls in white snowflakes. Water freezes into ice. It makes the ground slippery. We can have fun building snowmen in the frost and snow.

Weather: Storm

In a **storm** there are very strong winds and lots of rain. Sometimes the sky is black. There is thunder and lightning. The thunder makes a loud noise and the lightning flashes in the sky.

Time

8.00
eight o'clock

8.15
quarter past eight

8.30
half past eight

8.45
quarter to nine

Times of day

morning
afternoon
evening
night

Days of the week

Monday
Tuesday
Wednesday
Thursday
Friday
Saturday
Sunday